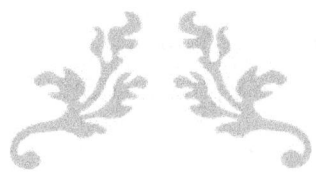

HOW I MADE MY 1 MILLION DOLLARS IN A YEAR?

The Secret About Private Equity That's Invested by the Rich

Patrick Lim

Table of Contents

COPYRIGHT 3

ABOUT THE AUTHOR 4

Chapter One 5

My 1 Million Journey 5

   Personal journey & how private equity played a key role 5

   The secret the rich use to grow wealth fast 7

   Conclusion 9

Chapter Two 10

Private Equity – The Secret Weapon of the Wealthy 10

   Understanding Private Equity 10

   Differences from Public Markets 11

   The Exclusivity Factor 12

   Why the Rich Invest in Private Equity 12

   Case Study: The Rothschild Family 14

   Conclusion 15

Chapter Three 16

Starting Small and Scaling Fast 16

   How to Make Your First Private Equity Investment 16

   Scaling from $100K to $1M Through Smart, Calculated Risks
.... 18

   Conclusion 19

Chapter Four 20

High Returns, Managed Risks 20

   How Private Equity Balances Risk and Reward 20

Case Studies of Wealth Creation Through Private Equity 22

Conclusion 23

Chapter Five 25

Breaking Barriers – Accessing Private Equity 25

Understanding the Barriers to Entry 25

Overcoming Barriers to Entry 26

New Ways for Regular Investors to Participate 28

Conclusion 29

Chapter Six 31

My Million-Dollar Secrets – Applying Private Equity to Your Wealth Journey 31

Recap of the Key Lessons Learned on the Journey to 1 Million 31

Practical Steps for Readers to Take Action and Start Their Own Private Equity Journey 33

How Private Equity Can Be a Cornerstone of Building Long-Term Wealth 34

Conclusion 35

Chapter Seven 36

Conclusion: Your Path to Wealth through Private Equity 36

Key Takeaways 36

Actionable Steps for Readers 37

The Power of Private Equity in Long-Term Wealth Building .. 38

COPYRIGHT

HOW I MADE MY 1 MILLION DOLLARS IN A YEAR

Copyright © 2024 by Patrick Lim.

All rights reserved. No part of this book may be reproduced, stored in a retrieval system, or transmitted in any form or by any means, electronic, mechanical, photocopying, recording, scanning, or otherwise, without the prior written permission of the publisher.

Any references to historical events, real people, or real places are used fictiously. Names, characters, and places are products of the author's imagination.

Published by Kindle Direct Publishing, in the United States of America.

First printing edition Oct 11, 2024.

Printed by Amazon.com Services LLC,

Monee, IL, USA

ABOUT THE AUTHOR

HOW I MADE MY 1 MILLION DOLLARS IN A YEAR

My name is Patrick Lim, and I am the CEO of a licensed fund management company in Singapore, which I founded in 2017. I'm also a Chartered Financial Consultant (ChFC/S) with a deep passion for helping others navigate the financial landscape.

My financial journey began in 2014 through forex trading. While I made part of my wealth in this fast-paced arena, I quickly realized that successful trading required extensive monitoring of the market and precise timing—challenges that often left little room for flexibility. This experience taught me invaluable lessons about risk management and market dynamics, but it also led me to seek out more stable and rewarding investment avenues.

As I transitioned into alternative investments, I discovered the world of private equity. This shift allowed me to leverage my skills and experience to explore high-growth opportunities that many investors often overlook.

In this book, "How I Made My 1 Million Dollars in a Year," I share my personal journey and the strategies that propelled me to financial success. Whether you're a seasoned investor or just starting out, my insights into private equity will help you understand how to replicate my achievements and build lasting wealth.

Chapter One

My 1 Million Journey

Personal journey & how private equity played a key role

When I set the goal of making $1 million within a year, I knew it would take more than just traditional investing. I needed to tap into opportunities that offered higher returns in shorter timeframes. That's when I turned to private equity—a world typically dominated by the wealthy, where high-risk investments can lead to life-changing returns.

I started with $300,000, carefully choosing where to allocate my capital. I knew I had to be smart, and I needed to get into the right deals. After months of research and connecting with the right networks, I made two key investments that became the pillars of my success.

The first win came when I put $50,000 into an online gaming company focused on esports. Esports was growing rapidly, and I saw potential in the company's platform for competitive gaming. The risk was high, but I believed in their business model and the explosive growth of the industry. A few months later, the company had a successful exit, and my investment turned into $350,000—a 7X return. This was the moment I realized that private equity, when done right, could create wealth far beyond what traditional investments could offer.

My second win came shortly after. I invested another $50,000 in a quantum computing company that was preparing for its pre-IPO round in the U.S. Quantum computing was a frontier technology, and although it was speculative, I felt the company had the right team and vision to make a breakthrough. Just months later, the company went public, and my $50,000 turned into $175,000, giving me a 3.5X return in a very short period.

With these two investments alone, I had turned $100,000 into $525,000. The remaining $200,000 was spread across other private equity opportunities, some of which are still maturing. But thanks to these early wins, I hit the $1 million mark within the year.

This wasn't just luck. It was about understanding the private equity market, identifying high-growth sectors like esports and quantum computing, and taking calculated risks. My journey to $1M was built on the same principles that the rich use to grow their wealth—accessing exclusive deals, leveraging patience, and making strategic investments.

In this book, I'll take you through the exact steps I took, sharing the secrets of private equity that the wealthy use to multiply their wealth. You don't need millions to get started, but you do need the right knowledge and mindset. Let's dive in.

The secret the rich use to grow wealth fast

When it comes to building wealth, the wealthy have access to tools and strategies that often remain hidden from the average investor. These secrets aren't about taking wild risks or chasing fleeting trends; rather, they involve disciplined approaches, strategic decision-making, and a deep understanding of the investment landscape. In this section, I'll uncover some of the key strategies that the rich utilize to accelerate their wealth-building journey.

1. Investing in Private Equity

One of the most powerful secrets the rich use is investing in private equity. Unlike traditional investments, private equity offers high returns through investments in privately held companies, often at early growth stages. The wealthy understand that while these investments carry risks, the potential for significant gains is unmatched. They leverage their connections to access exclusive deals and opportunities that the average investor may never see.

2. Diversification Across Asset Classes

The wealthy know the importance of diversification, not just within a single asset class but across multiple asset classes. This includes real estate, stocks, bonds, and alternative investments like private equity and venture capital. By spreading their investments, they minimize risk and create multiple streams of income. This diversified approach not only protects their capital but also enhances their potential for growth.

3. Long-Term Thinking and Patience

While many investors seek quick wins, the rich take a long-term perspective. They understand that wealth accumulation often takes time and that compounding returns can lead to exponential growth. By investing in businesses or assets with strong fundamentals, they allow their investments to grow organically over time, reaping the rewards of patience and discipline.

4. Networking and Relationships

The wealthy recognize that relationships can be just as valuable as capital. They build extensive networks of like-minded investors, industry experts, and mentors who can provide insights, opportunities, and guidance. By leveraging these relationships, they gain access to exclusive deals and valuable knowledge that can significantly enhance their investment strategies.

5. Continuous Learning and Adaptation

The financial landscape is constantly evolving, and the wealthy stay ahead by committing to lifelong learning. They keep abreast of market trends, economic shifts, and emerging technologies that could impact their investments. By adapting their strategies and remaining open to new ideas, they position themselves to seize opportunities that others might miss.

6. Leveraging Debt Wisely

Another secret the wealthy use is the strategic use of debt. While many people fear debt, the rich understand that it can be a powerful tool when used wisely. By leveraging debt to finance investments, they can amplify their returns without tying up all their capital. This approach requires careful management, but when executed correctly, it can lead to significant wealth accumulation.

Conclusion

These strategies are just a glimpse into the world of wealth-building that the rich navigate every day. In this book, I will delve deeper into these principles and share how I applied them on my journey to making 1 million dollars in a year. By understanding and implementing these secrets, you too can harness the power of private equity and unlock your financial potential. Let's embark on this journey together and uncover the pathways to your financial success.

Chapter Two

Private Equity – The Secret Weapon of the Wealthy

Private equity refers to investments made in companies that are not publicly traded on a stock exchange. These investments typically involve acquiring a significant stake in a company, with the goal of improving its operations, increasing its value, and eventually exiting the investment at a profit, often through a sale or public offering. The appeal of private equity lies in its potential for high returns, which often far exceed those available in traditional public markets.

Understanding Private Equity

Private equity can take many forms, including:

1. **Buyouts:** Acquiring a controlling interest in a company, often to restructure or improve its performance.

2. **Venture Capital:** Investing in early-stage companies with high growth potential, typically in exchange for equity.

3. **Growth Capital:** Investing in established companies that need funding for expansion or to enter new markets.

4. **Distressed Assets:** Purchasing undervalued or troubled companies with the intention of turning them around.

Private equity firms pool capital from investors—such as wealthy individuals, pension funds, and institutional investors—to create funds that target specific industries or types of companies. These firms typically have specialized knowledge and experience in managing and growing businesses, which gives them a competitive advantage in identifying profitable opportunities.

Differences from Public Markets

1. **Liquidity:** Public market investments, such as stocks, can be bought and sold quickly, providing investors with liquidity. In contrast, private equity investments are illiquid, meaning that capital is usually tied up for several years until the investment matures or an exit occurs. This illiquidity can be a disadvantage for some investors, but it allows private equity firms to focus on long-term value creation without the pressure of short-term market fluctuations.

2. **Valuation Methods:** Public companies are valued based on market sentiment and trading activity, often influenced by short-term performance metrics. Private equity firms use different valuation methods, focusing on intrinsic value, operational performance, and long-term growth potential. This approach enables them to identify undervalued companies that may not be reflected in public market prices.

3. **Regulatory Environment:** Public companies must adhere to strict regulatory requirements, including regular financial reporting and disclosures. Private equity investments, on the other hand, face fewer regulations, allowing for more flexibility in operations and decision-making. This less regulated environment can create

opportunities for private equity firms to implement changes more rapidly than their public counterparts.

4. **Control and Influence:** Private equity investors typically have a more significant level of control over the companies they invest in, often taking seats on the board and actively participating in management decisions. This contrasts with public market investors, who generally have little influence over corporate governance.

The Exclusivity Factor

One of the defining characteristics of private equity is its exclusivity. Access to private equity investments is often limited to accredited investors, institutions, and high-net-worth individuals due to the substantial capital requirements and the complexities involved in these deals. This exclusivity creates a barrier to entry for average investors, making private equity a space where the wealthy can leverage their resources for potentially outsized gains.

The ability to invest in private equity opportunities often depends on networking and building relationships with fund managers and industry insiders. As a result, those within affluent circles are more likely to discover and access lucrative investment opportunities, further amplifying the wealth gap between the rich and the average investor.

Why the Rich Invest in Private Equity

1. **Higher Potential Returns:** One of the primary reasons the wealthy flock to private equity is the potential for higher returns compared to public markets. While stock market investments might yield average annual returns of 7-10%, private equity can offer returns of 20% or more, especially when investing in high-growth sectors.

2. **Access to Exclusive Opportunities:** Private equity investments often require substantial capital and are usually limited to accredited or institutional investors. This exclusivity means that those with wealth can access deals that are not available to the general public, giving them a distinct advantage in building their portfolios.

3. **Active Management and Control:** Private equity investors typically take an active role in managing the companies they invest in. This level of involvement allows them to implement strategic changes, drive operational efficiencies, and ultimately increase the value of their investments.

4. **Diversification:** Investing in private equity provides diversification beyond traditional stocks and bonds. By including private equity in their portfolios, wealthy investors can reduce overall risk while enhancing potential returns.

5. **Tax Advantages:** Depending on the jurisdiction, private equity investments may offer tax benefits that can significantly enhance net returns. For example, long-term capital gains tax rates can be lower than ordinary income tax rates, allowing investors to retain more of their profits.

6. **Long-Term Growth:** Wealthy investors often have a long-term investment horizon, allowing them to weather

short-term market fluctuations. Private equity investments are typically illiquid and require a longer commitment, aligning well with the long-term growth strategies of affluent individuals.

Case Study: The Rothschild Family

The Rothschild family is a prime example of how investing in private equity can lead to extraordinary wealth accumulation. Originating in the late 18th century, the Rothschilds established themselves as one of the most prominent banking families in Europe. Their success was not merely a result of banking; they were also adept at investing in various industries, including mining, railroads, and agriculture.

One of the family's notable strategies involved investing in emerging markets and industries. For instance, in the 19th century, they made substantial investments in railways across Europe and the Americas, capitalizing on the rapid industrialization of the era. These investments not only yielded significant returns but also positioned the Rothschilds as influential players in shaping the modern economy.

The Rothschilds further diversified their investments by creating a network of partnerships and alliances across different sectors and geographies. This approach allowed them to access exclusive investment opportunities, much like modern private equity firms do today. Their ability to identify undervalued assets and invest in growth sectors exemplifies the long-term thinking and strategic decision-making that characterize successful private equity investing.

Even in contemporary times, the Rothschild family continues to leverage their expertise in private equity, focusing on industries such as renewable energy, real estate, and technology. Their enduring success serves as a testament to the effectiveness of private equity as a wealth-building strategy.

Conclusion

Private equity represents a powerful avenue for wealth creation, allowing investors to leverage their capital in ways that traditional markets cannot. The differences between private equity and public markets, along with the exclusivity factor, highlight why the rich are drawn to this investment space. In the following chapters, I will share my personal experiences in private equity, the strategies I employed, and the insights I gained along the way. Understanding what private equity is and why the rich invest in it is the first step toward replicating their success in your own financial journey.

Chapter Three

Starting Small and Scaling Fast

The journey into private equity can seem daunting, especially for newcomers without substantial capital or experience. However, the beauty of this investment avenue is that you don't need to start with millions to make a significant impact. In this chapter, I will guide you through how to make your first private equity investment, emphasizing the importance of starting small and scaling up through smart, calculated risks.

How to Make Your First Private Equity Investment

1. **Educate Yourself**: Before diving into private equity, it's essential to understand the fundamentals of the market. Familiarize yourself with different types of investments, such as venture capital, growth equity, and buyouts. Read books, attend seminars, and network with industry professionals to build a solid foundation of knowledge.

2. **Identify Your Investment Criteria**: Determine what types of companies or sectors you want to invest in. Are you interested in tech startups, healthcare, or sustainable energy? Define your criteria based on factors such as industry trends, market size, and potential for growth. This focus will help streamline your search for investment opportunities.

3. **Network and Build Relationships**: Networking is crucial in private equity. Attend industry conferences, join

investment clubs, and connect with professionals on platforms like LinkedIn. Building relationships with venture capitalists, fund managers, and entrepreneurs can provide you with valuable insights and access to exclusive deals.

4. **Start with a Fund**: For first-time investors, participating in a private equity fund can be a prudent way to enter the market. Funds allow you to pool resources with other investors, spreading the risk and providing access to a diversified portfolio. Look for reputable funds with a track record of success, and ensure they align with your investment goals.

5. **Consider Angel Investing**: If you're inclined towards direct investments, consider starting with angel investing. This involves providing capital to early-stage startups in exchange for equity. While riskier, angel investing can offer substantial returns if you choose the right company. Conduct thorough due diligence on potential investments and seek guidance from experienced investors.

6. **Start Small**: Your first investment doesn't need to be large. Begin with a manageable amount—say, $50,000 to $100,000. This allows you to gain experience without overexposing yourself financially. As you become more comfortable and knowledgeable in the private equity space, you can gradually increase your investment amounts.

Scaling from $100K to $1M Through Smart, Calculated Risks

Once you've made your initial investment, the key to scaling your capital lies in adopting a strategic approach to risk management.

1. **Assessing Risk vs. Reward**: Each investment carries inherent risks, but successful investors understand the relationship between risk and potential returns. When considering new opportunities, evaluate the risks involved and determine if they align with your overall investment strategy. Prioritize investments that offer a favorable risk-to-reward ratio.

2. **Diversify Your Portfolio**: As you accumulate wealth, diversification becomes critical. Allocate your capital across various sectors and investment stages to mitigate risk. A diversified portfolio can withstand market fluctuations and enhance your chances of achieving consistent returns. Consider a mix of established companies and high-potential startups to balance risk and growth.

3. **Reinvest Profits**: Instead of cashing out your profits, reinvest them into new opportunities. This strategy can accelerate your wealth-building journey through the power of compounding. For instance, if your initial $100,000 investment yields a return of 7X, reinvesting the $700,000 can open doors to even larger investment opportunities.

4. **Seek High-Impact Opportunities**: As you gain experience, focus on high-impact investment opportunities that can significantly boost your portfolio.

Look for industries poised for rapid growth or companies with disruptive technologies. Stay informed about market trends and emerging sectors that could present lucrative investment possibilities.

5. **Leverage Expertise**: As you scale your investments, consider partnering with experienced advisors or fund managers. Their insights and expertise can help you identify high-potential investments and navigate complex deals. Additionally, mentorship from seasoned investors can provide invaluable guidance as you progress on your investment journey.

6. **Be Patient and Persistent**: Scaling from $100K to $1M will not happen overnight. Successful private equity investing requires patience and a long-term perspective. Market fluctuations and economic conditions may affect your investments, but maintaining focus on your long-term goals will pay off in the end.

Conclusion

Starting small and scaling fast is not only feasible in private equity; it's a proven path to building substantial wealth. By educating yourself, networking, and taking calculated risks, you can navigate this complex investment landscape and achieve significant returns. In the subsequent chapters, I will share my personal experiences and insights that helped me scale my investments, ultimately leading to my journey of making $1 million within a year. Embrace the process, learn from each experience, and let your journey in private equity unfold.

Chapter Four

High Returns, Managed Risks

Private equity is often touted for its potential to deliver extraordinary returns, making it an attractive investment avenue for the wealthy. However, the inherent risks associated with these investments cannot be overlooked. In this chapter, we will explore how private equity balances risk and reward, providing insights into the strategies employed by successful investors. Additionally, I will present case studies that illustrate wealth creation through private equity, highlighting how calculated risks can lead to substantial gains.

How Private Equity Balances Risk and Reward

1. **Thorough Due Diligence**: One of the key strategies private equity firms employ to manage risk is rigorous due diligence. This process involves a comprehensive analysis of potential investments, including financial health, market position, management team, and growth prospects. By thoroughly vetting opportunities, private equity firms can identify red flags and make informed investment decisions, thereby minimizing potential losses.

2. **Active Management**: Unlike passive investment strategies, private equity investors often take an active role in managing their portfolio companies. This involvement allows them to implement strategic changes, optimize operations, and drive growth. By

being hands-on, private equity firms can mitigate risks associated with underperforming assets and enhance overall portfolio performance.

3. **Diversification**: Diversification is a fundamental principle in investment management, and private equity is no exception. By spreading investments across different sectors, stages of growth, and geographies, private equity firms can reduce the impact of a single investment's poor performance on the overall portfolio. This strategic allocation of capital helps balance the risk-reward equation.

4. **Structured Financing**: Private equity firms often use a mix of debt and equity to finance their acquisitions. While leveraging debt can amplify returns, it also introduces additional risk. However, by employing structured financing techniques, private equity firms can optimize their capital structure, ensuring that the potential rewards outweigh the risks involved.

5. **Exit Strategies**: Private equity investments are typically long-term commitments, but successful firms have clear exit strategies in place. These may include selling the company to a strategic buyer, taking it public through an IPO, or selling to another private equity firm. A well-defined exit strategy allows investors to maximize their returns while minimizing risk exposure during the investment horizon.

6. **Focus on Value Creation**: The ultimate goal of private equity is to create value within the companies they invest in. This value creation can take many forms, including operational improvements, market expansion, and strategic repositioning. By focusing on enhancing the

intrinsic value of portfolio companies, private equity investors can achieve superior returns while managing risk effectively.

Case Studies of Wealth Creation Through Private Equity

1. **The Carlyle Group and Booz Allen Hamilton**: The Carlyle Group, one of the world's largest private equity firms, acquired a majority stake in Booz Allen Hamilton in 2008. The firm recognized the potential for growth in the consulting sector, particularly in government services. Through strategic management and operational improvements, Carlyle was able to increase Booz Allen's revenues and profitability. In 2010, Booz Allen went public, and the IPO was highly successful, resulting in significant returns for Carlyle and its investors. This case exemplifies how private equity can create wealth by identifying high-potential companies and executing effective growth strategies.

2. **Sequoia Capital and Apple**: While primarily known as a venture capital firm, Sequoia Capital's early investment in Apple in the late 1970s is a classic example of wealth creation through private equity principles. Sequoia recognized Apple's innovative potential and invested $150,000 in the company during its formative years. As Apple grew and transformed into a tech giant, Sequoia's investment multiplied exponentially. The success of this investment underscores the importance of identifying visionary companies and being willing to take calculated risks on their growth trajectories.

3. **Blackstone and Hilton Worldwide**: In 2007, Blackstone acquired Hilton Worldwide for approximately $26 billion, making it one of the largest leveraged buyouts in history. At the time, Hilton faced challenges due to the economic downturn, but Blackstone saw potential for recovery and growth. Through effective management and strategic investments in expanding Hilton's portfolio, Blackstone repositioned the company. By 2013, Hilton went public in a highly successful IPO, resulting in substantial returns for Blackstone and its investors. This case illustrates how private equity can successfully navigate economic challenges and drive value creation through strategic foresight.

4. **KKR and Dollar General**: KKR acquired Dollar General in 2007, recognizing the potential for growth in the discount retail sector. The firm focused on operational improvements and expanding Dollar General's store footprint. Under KKR's management, Dollar General experienced significant revenue growth and increased profitability. In 2011, KKR took Dollar General public, and the IPO was a resounding success, providing KKR and its investors with substantial returns. This example demonstrates how private equity can leverage market trends and operational expertise to drive wealth creation.

Conclusion

The balance of risk and reward in private equity is not left to chance; it is the result of strategic planning, active management, and rigorous analysis. By employing thorough due diligence, diversifying investments, and focusing on value creation, private equity investors can achieve exceptional returns while effectively managing risks. The case studies presented in this chapter highlight real-world examples of wealth creation through private equity, underscoring the potential for significant financial success. In the next chapter, we will delve into specific strategies and techniques for identifying high-potential investment opportunities, helping you navigate the private equity landscape with confidence.

Chapter Five

Breaking Barriers – Accessing Private Equity

Private equity has long been viewed as an exclusive domain reserved for wealthy individuals, institutional investors, and sophisticated fund managers. However, the landscape is evolving, and new opportunities are emerging that allow regular investors to participate in this lucrative asset class. In this chapter, we will explore how to overcome the high barriers to entry in private equity and discuss innovative ways that everyday investors can access and benefit from these investment opportunities.

Understanding the Barriers to Entry

Before diving into how to overcome these barriers, it's essential to understand what they are:

1. **Accredited Investor Requirements**: Many private equity funds require investors to be accredited, meaning they must meet specific income or net worth thresholds. This requirement effectively excludes a large portion of the population from investing in these funds.

2. **High Minimum Investment Amounts**: Private equity investments typically come with high minimum investment amounts, often ranging from $250,000 to $1 million. This level of capital can be prohibitive for many individual investors.

3. **Illiquidity**: Private equity investments are generally illiquid, requiring investors to commit their capital for several years without the ability to access it. This lack of liquidity can deter potential investors who prefer more flexible investment options.

4. **Complexity of Investments**: The intricacies of private equity investments, including deal structures, valuations, and operational management, can be daunting for those without a financial background. This complexity can create a barrier for regular investors seeking to participate.

Overcoming Barriers to Entry

1. **Education and Awareness**: The first step in overcoming barriers to entry is education. Aspiring investors should take the time to understand the fundamentals of private equity, including the different investment structures, risks, and rewards. Numerous online courses, webinars, and resources are available to help build financial literacy and demystify the private equity landscape.

2. **Leverage Crowdfunding Platforms**: One of the most significant developments in recent years is the rise of crowdfunding platforms that focus on private equity investments. These platforms allow individuals to invest in startups and private companies with lower minimum investment requirements. Platforms like EquityZen, SeedInvest, and Crowdcube provide opportunities for regular investors to access private equity deals, often with minimums as low as $1,000 to $10,000.

3. **Participate in Private Equity Funds of Funds**: Another way to access private equity is through funds of funds. These funds pool capital from multiple investors and then invest in various private equity funds. By participating in a fund of funds, investors can gain exposure to a diversified portfolio of private equity investments while meeting lower minimum investment thresholds than direct investment in a single fund.

4. **Utilize Exchange-Traded Funds (ETFs) and Mutual Funds**: Several ETFs and mutual funds now provide exposure to private equity investments. These investment vehicles allow individual investors to gain access to private equity markets without having to meet accredited investor requirements or commit large amounts of capital. While the returns may not match those of direct private equity investments, they offer a more accessible entry point for regular investors.

5. **Seek Out Angel Investing Networks**: Angel investing networks provide a platform for individuals to pool their resources and invest in early-stage startups. Many of these networks welcome non-accredited investors, allowing them to participate in private equity investments that were once reserved for the wealthy. Joining an angel investing group can provide valuable learning opportunities and access to a variety of investment opportunities.

6. **Collaborate with Financial Advisors**: Engaging with a financial advisor who specializes in alternative investments can help regular investors navigate the complexities of private equity. These professionals can provide insights into suitable investment opportunities

and help build a diversified portfolio that includes private equity.

7. **Stay Informed About Regulatory Changes**: The regulatory landscape surrounding private equity is continuously evolving. Stay informed about changes in laws and regulations that may open up new investment opportunities for non-accredited investors. The Jumpstart Our Business Startups (JOBS) Act in the U.S., for example, has expanded access to private investments for everyday investors, and similar initiatives may emerge in other jurisdictions.

New Ways for Regular Investors to Participate

1. **Equity Crowdfunding**: Platforms that facilitate equity crowdfunding allow regular investors to buy equity stakes in startups and small businesses. This model not only democratizes access to private equity but also enables investors to support innovative companies and entrepreneurs. Examples include Wefunder and StartEngine, which provide diverse investment opportunities across various sectors.

2. **Real Estate Investment Trusts (REITs)**: While traditional REITs invest in publicly traded real estate, some private equity firms have started offering private REITs that focus on private real estate investments. These REITs can provide access to private equity-like returns while allowing investors to benefit from real estate without the need for significant capital.

3. **Secondary Marketplaces**: As the private equity landscape evolves, secondary marketplaces are emerging where investors can buy and sell stakes in private equity funds. These platforms, such as Forge Global and EquityZen, provide liquidity and enable investors to exit their investments earlier than the typical private equity holding period.

4. **Direct Investment Platforms**: Some online platforms enable individual investors to participate directly in private equity deals. Companies like AngelList and FundersClub allow investors to choose specific startups or private companies to invest in, often with lower minimum investments than traditional private equity funds.

5. **Tokenization of Assets**: The concept of tokenization—representing ownership of real-world assets on a blockchain—has gained traction in private equity. This innovation allows investors to purchase fractional ownership in private companies or funds through digital tokens, lowering barriers to entry and enhancing liquidity.

Conclusion

Breaking the barriers to access private equity is essential for creating a more inclusive investment landscape. By leveraging new platforms, networks, and investment vehicles, regular investors can tap into the wealth-building potential of private equity. As the market continues to evolve, it is crucial for aspiring investors to stay informed and take advantage of these emerging opportunities. In the next chapter, we will explore the key factors to consider when evaluating private equity investments, equipping you with the tools to make informed decisions in your investment journey.

Chapter Six

My Million-Dollar Secrets – Applying Private Equity to Your Wealth Journey

Achieving a million-dollar milestone is not just about luck; it's a culmination of strategic planning, informed decision-making, and the willingness to take calculated risks. As I reflect on my journey to making $1 million within a year, I want to share the key lessons I've learned along the way. In this chapter, I will outline practical steps you can take to embark on your own private equity journey and explain how private equity can serve as a cornerstone for building long-term wealth.

Recap of the Key Lessons Learned on the Journey to 1 Million

1. **Start with Education**: Knowledge is power, especially in private equity. Understanding the fundamentals of investing, market dynamics, and specific sectors can significantly enhance your investment decisions. Take the time to educate yourself through books, seminars, and networking with industry professionals.

2. **Embrace the Power of Networking**: Building relationships with other investors, fund managers, and entrepreneurs can open doors to new opportunities. Attend industry events, engage with online communities, and connect with mentors who can guide you in your private equity journey.

3. **Start Small and Scale Up**: You don't need a fortune to enter the private equity space. Begin with manageable investments, learn from your experiences, and gradually increase your exposure as you become more comfortable. This approach minimizes risk while allowing you to build confidence in your investment choices.

4. **Focus on Value Creation**: Successful private equity investing hinges on creating value within the companies you invest in. Whether through operational improvements, strategic repositioning, or market expansion, focus on enhancing the intrinsic value of your investments to achieve higher returns.

5. **Diversify Your Portfolio**: Don't put all your eggs in one basket. Diversifying your investments across different sectors and stages can mitigate risks and enhance your overall portfolio performance. A well-balanced portfolio is key to weathering market fluctuations.

6. **Leverage Technology and New Investment Avenues**: With the rise of crowdfunding platforms, funds of funds, and secondary marketplaces, accessing private equity has become more feasible than ever. Embrace these innovative avenues to participate in private equity investments, even with limited capital.

7. **Be Patient and Persistent**: Building wealth through private equity is a long-term endeavor. Stay focused on your goals, remain patient during market fluctuations, and persistently seek out new opportunities. The journey may be challenging, but the rewards can be substantial.

Practical Steps for Readers to Take Action and Start Their Own Private Equity Journey

1. **Assess Your Financial Situation**: Start by evaluating your current financial position. Determine how much capital you can allocate to private equity investments while maintaining a diversified portfolio. This assessment will help you set realistic investment goals.

2. **Educate Yourself**: Dedicate time to learning about private equity. Read books, take online courses, and engage with experts in the field. Knowledge will empower you to make informed decisions and navigate the complexities of private equity investing.

3. **Join Investment Networks**: Connect with like-minded investors by joining investment clubs or online communities focused on private equity. These networks can provide valuable insights, resources, and opportunities for collaboration.

4. **Identify Your Investment Criteria**: Define your investment strategy by identifying the types of companies or sectors you want to target. Develop a clear set of criteria to guide your investment decisions, helping you stay focused on your goals.

5. **Start Investing**: Begin your investment journey by participating in crowdfunding platforms, funds of funds, or other accessible investment vehicles. Starting with smaller amounts will allow you to learn and adapt your strategy as you gain experience.

6. **Monitor and Adjust Your Portfolio**: Regularly review your investments and adjust your portfolio as needed.

Stay informed about market trends, performance metrics, and economic indicators that may impact your investments. Adapt your strategy to capitalize on new opportunities.

7. **Reinvest Profits**: When you achieve gains from your investments, consider reinvesting those profits into new opportunities. Compounding your returns will accelerate your wealth-building journey and enhance your overall investment portfolio.

How Private Equity Can Be a Cornerstone of Building Long-Term Wealth

Private equity offers several advantages that make it a valuable component of a long-term wealth-building strategy:

1. **High Potential Returns**: Private equity investments have the potential to deliver superior returns compared to traditional asset classes, such as stocks and bonds. By focusing on value creation and growth, private equity investors can capitalize on lucrative opportunities.

2. **Diversification Benefits**: Including private equity in your investment portfolio can enhance diversification. The performance of private equity investments often differs from public markets, providing a buffer against market volatility and economic downturns.

3. **Access to Innovative Companies**: Private equity investors have the opportunity to invest in early-stage and innovative companies that may not yet be accessible in public markets. By participating in these investments,

you can support entrepreneurial ventures and benefit from their growth.

4. **Long-Term Growth Potential**: Private equity investments typically have longer holding periods, allowing for sustained growth and value creation over time. This long-term perspective aligns with the goal of building lasting wealth.

5. **Hands-On Engagement**: In many cases, private equity investors play an active role in managing their investments. This hands-on approach allows you to influence outcomes and drive value creation within portfolio companies.

Conclusion

As you embark on your private equity journey, remember that building wealth is a marathon, not a sprint. By applying the key lessons learned from my journey, taking practical steps, and recognizing the potential of private equity, you can establish a strong foundation for long-term financial success. Embrace the opportunities that lie ahead, stay committed to your goals, and leverage the power of private equity to achieve your wealth-building aspirations. Your journey begins now, and with dedication and the right strategies, you too can unlock the secrets to financial prosperity.

Chapter Seven

Conclusion: Your Path to Wealth through Private Equity

As we reach the end of this journey through the world of private equity, it's essential to consolidate the knowledge and insights gained along the way. The path to wealth through private equity is not just about making smart investments; it's about cultivating a mindset of continuous learning, strategic thinking, and proactive engagement in your financial future. This conclusion aims to summarize key takeaways and outline actionable steps for you as you embark on your own path to wealth.

Key Takeaways

1. **Education is Fundamental**: Knowledge is the bedrock of successful investing. Understanding the intricacies of private equity, including its structure, risks, and opportunities, will empower you to make informed decisions. Invest time in educating yourself and staying current with industry trends.

2. **Start Small and Scale**: Entering the private equity space doesn't require a massive capital outlay. Start with smaller investments to gain experience, learn the ropes, and gradually scale up as your confidence and understanding grow.

3. **Diversification is Key**: A well-diversified portfolio mitigates risks and enhances returns. By diversifying your

investments across sectors, stages, and geographies, you can better navigate market fluctuations and seize opportunities.

4. **Networking Matters**: Building relationships with fellow investors, fund managers, and industry experts can provide valuable insights and open doors to new opportunities. Engage with communities and networks to enhance your investment journey.

5. **Focus on Value Creation**: Successful private equity investing is centered on creating value within portfolio companies. Whether through operational improvements or strategic growth initiatives, prioritize investments that have clear potential for value enhancement.

6. **Utilize Modern Investment Avenues**: With the rise of crowdfunding platforms, funds of funds, and secondary markets, accessing private equity is more feasible than ever. Embrace these innovative avenues to diversify your investment portfolio and unlock new opportunities.

7. **Be Patient and Persistent**: Wealth-building through private equity is a long-term endeavor. Stay committed to your goals, be patient during market fluctuations, and persistently seek new investment opportunities. The rewards of your efforts will compound over time.

Actionable Steps for Readers

1. **Create an Investment Plan**: Start by outlining your investment goals, risk tolerance, and capital allocation

strategy. Define your target sectors and the types of private equity investments you wish to pursue.

2. **Educate Yourself**: Commit to continuous learning by reading books, attending workshops, and engaging with experienced investors. Consider enrolling in courses specifically focused on private equity and alternative investments.

3. **Join Investment Networks**: Connect with local or online investment groups focused on private equity. Sharing experiences and insights with like-minded individuals can enhance your knowledge and investment acumen.

4. **Take the First Step**: Begin investing by utilizing accessible platforms that allow for smaller investment amounts. Whether through crowdfunding or funds of funds, take that first step toward your private equity journey.

5. **Monitor and Adjust**: Regularly review your investment portfolio to assess performance and make adjustments as needed. Stay informed about market trends and adapt your strategy based on new insights.

6. **Reinvest Profits**: As you achieve returns from your investments, consider reinvesting those profits to take advantage of compounding growth. This strategy will accelerate your wealth-building journey.

The Power of Private Equity in Long-Term Wealth Building

Private equity is a powerful tool for wealth building, offering the potential for high returns, diversification benefits, and access to innovative companies. By taking a proactive approach to your financial journey and applying the lessons learned in this book, you can leverage private equity as a cornerstone of your long-term wealth strategy.

As you move forward, remember that success in private equity, like any investment endeavor, requires a combination of knowledge, discipline, and a commitment to continuous improvement. Embrace the opportunities that lie ahead, stay focused on your goals, and let private equity be a vital part of your path to financial prosperity.

Your journey to wealth through private equity begins now—take the first step and unlock the secrets to building a brighter financial future.

End.

www.ingramcontent.com/pod-product-compliance
Lightning Source LLC
Chambersburg PA
CBHW070954220526
45471CB00007B/3028